50 Global Grilling Galore Recipes for Home

By: Kelly Johnson

Table of Contents

- Argentine Grilled Chimichurri Steak
- Korean BBQ Bulgogi
- Jamaican Jerk Chicken
- Brazilian Churrasco Skewers
- Moroccan Spiced Lamb Kebabs
- Greek Souvlaki with Tzatziki
- Hawaiian Huli Huli Chicken
- Mexican Carne Asada Tacos
- Indian Tandoori Chicken
- Turkish Adana Kebabs
- Thai Grilled Lemongrass Pork
- Peruvian Anticuchos (Grilled Beef Heart)
- Italian Grilled Bruschetta Chicken
- South African Boerewors Sausage
- Spanish Grilled Seafood Paella
- Filipino Inihaw na Baboy (Grilled Pork Belly)
- Lebanese Grilled Kafta Kebabs
- Chinese Char Siu Pork
- Australian Grilled Kangaroo
- Vietnamese Grilled Lemongrass Beef
- Russian Shashlik (Marinated Grilled Skewers)
- Jamaican Escovitch Fish
- Argentine Provoleta (Grilled Cheese)
- Mexican Street Corn (Elote)
- Greek Grilled Halloumi Cheese
- Brazilian Picanha Steak
- Thai Grilled Coconut Milk Marinated Chicken
- Turkish Grilled Eggplant Kebabs
- Korean Grilled Miso-Glazed Salmon
- Indian Grilled Paneer Tikka
- Peruvian Grilled Chicken with Aji Verde
- Moroccan Grilled Vegetable Platter
- Italian Grilled Octopus
- South African Braai Broodjie (Grilled Cheese Sandwich)
- Spanish Grilled Piquillo Peppers

- Filipino Bangus (Grilled Milkfish)
- Lebanese Grilled Garlic Shrimp
- Chinese Grilled Eggplant with Garlic Sauce
- Australian Grilled Barramundi
- Vietnamese Grilled Pork Banh Mi
- Russian Grilled Potatoes with Dill
- Jamaican Grilled Jerk Portobello Mushrooms
- Argentine Grilled Sausage with Chimichurri
- Greek Grilled Feta with Honey
- Turkish Grilled Quail
- Korean Grilled Gochujang Ribs
- Italian Grilled Swordfish with Lemon
- Brazilian Grilled Pineapple with Cinnamon
- Indian Grilled Tandoori Naan
- Thai Grilled Green Curry Chicken Skewers

Argentine Grilled Chimichurri Steak

Ingredients:

For the Steak:

- 2 pounds flank steak or skirt steak
- Salt and black pepper to taste
- 2 tablespoons olive oil

For the Chimichurri Sauce:

- 1 cup fresh parsley, finely chopped
- 1/4 cup fresh oregano, finely chopped
- 4 cloves garlic, minced
- 1/2 cup red wine vinegar
- 1/2 cup extra virgin olive oil
- 1 teaspoon red pepper flakes (adjust to taste)
- Salt and black pepper to taste

Instructions:

1. Preheat the Grill:

- Preheat your grill to medium-high heat.

2. Season the Steak:

- Pat the steak dry with paper towels and season both sides generously with salt and black pepper. Drizzle the olive oil over the steak and rub it evenly.

3. Grill the Steak:

- Place the seasoned steak on the preheated grill. Cook for 4-5 minutes per side for medium-rare, or adjust the cooking time based on your desired doneness.
- Let the steak rest for a few minutes before slicing. This allows the juices to redistribute, keeping the meat tender.

4. Prepare the Chimichurri Sauce:

- While the steak is grilling, prepare the chimichurri sauce. In a bowl, combine the finely chopped parsley, oregano, minced garlic, red wine vinegar, extra virgin olive oil, red pepper flakes, salt, and black pepper. Mix well.
- Taste and adjust the seasonings according to your preference. If you like it spicier, you can add more red pepper flakes.

5. Slice and Serve:

- Once the steak has rested, slice it against the grain into thin strips.
- Serve the grilled steak on a platter and drizzle the chimichurri sauce generously over the top.

6. Enjoy:

- Enjoy your Argentine Grilled Chimichurri Steak with your favorite side dishes or as part of a traditional Argentine asado (barbecue) experience.

This dish captures the essence of Argentine cuisine with its perfectly grilled steak and the bold, herbaceous flavors of chimichurri sauce. It's a fantastic choice for a barbecue or any special occasion where you want to impress with authentic Argentine flavors.

Korean BBQ Bulgogi

Ingredients:

For the Marinade:

- 1.5 to 2 pounds thinly sliced beef (ribeye or sirloin works well)
- 1/2 cup soy sauce
- 1/4 cup sugar (white or brown)
- 3 tablespoons mirin (or rice wine)
- 3 tablespoons sesame oil
- 4 cloves garlic, minced
- 1 small onion, grated
- 1 pear, grated (or 1/2 cup unsweetened pear juice)
- 1 teaspoon grated ginger
- 1/4 teaspoon black pepper
- 2 green onions, finely chopped (for garnish)

For Serving:

- Cooked white rice
- Lettuce leaves (for wrapping, optional)
- Ssamjang (Korean dipping sauce, optional)
- Sesame seeds (for garnish)

Instructions:

1. Prepare the Marinade:

- In a bowl, combine soy sauce, sugar, mirin, sesame oil, minced garlic, grated onion, grated pear, grated ginger, and black pepper. Mix well until the sugar dissolves.

2. Marinate the Beef:

- Place the thinly sliced beef in a shallow dish or a resealable plastic bag.
- Pour the marinade over the beef, ensuring all slices are well coated. Massage the meat to evenly distribute the marinade.
- Seal the dish or bag and refrigerate for at least 1-2 hours, or preferably overnight, to allow the flavors to penetrate the meat.

3. Cook the Bulgogi:

- Heat a grill or grill pan over medium-high heat. Brush with a bit of oil to prevent sticking.
- Grill the marinated beef slices for 2-3 minutes on each side, or until cooked to your desired doneness.
- Alternatively, you can pan-fry the beef in a hot skillet until browned and cooked through.

4. Serve:

- Transfer the grilled bulgogi to a serving plate.
- Garnish with chopped green onions and sesame seeds.

5. Assemble:

- Serve the Korean BBQ Bulgogi with cooked white rice.
- Optionally, provide lettuce leaves for wrapping and offer ssamjang (Korean dipping sauce) on the side.

6. Enjoy:

- Enjoy the delicious Korean BBQ Bulgogi as a main dish, in lettuce wraps, or with your preferred accompaniments!

This Korean BBQ Bulgogi recipe offers a perfect balance of sweet and savory flavors, creating a mouthwatering dish that's sure to be a hit. Whether you're grilling outdoors or using a grill pan indoors, the result is a delightful and authentic Korean BBQ experience.

Jamaican Jerk Chicken

Ingredients:

For the Jerk Marinade:

- 3 green onions, chopped
- 3-4 Scotch bonnet peppers (adjust for spice preference), seeds removed and chopped
- 1 tablespoon fresh thyme leaves
- 2 teaspoons ground allspice
- 1 teaspoon ground cinnamon
- 1 teaspoon ground nutmeg
- 2 tablespoons soy sauce
- 2 tablespoons vegetable oil
- 1 tablespoon brown sugar
- 4 cloves garlic, minced
- 1 tablespoon fresh ginger, grated
- Juice of 2 limes
- Salt and black pepper to taste

For the Chicken:

- 4-6 chicken leg quarters or your preferred cuts

Instructions:

1. Prepare the Jerk Marinade:

- In a food processor or blender, combine all the jerk marinade ingredients. Blend until you get a smooth paste.

2. Marinate the Chicken:

- Place the chicken pieces in a large bowl or resealable plastic bag.
- Pour the jerk marinade over the chicken, ensuring it's well-coated. Use gloves when handling the Scotch bonnet peppers to avoid irritation.

- Massage the marinade into the chicken, making sure it gets under the skin for maximum flavor. Marinate in the refrigerator for at least 4 hours, preferably overnight.

3. Preheat the Grill:

- Preheat your grill to medium-high heat.

4. Grill the Chicken:

- Remove the chicken from the marinade, letting any excess drip off.
- Grill the chicken pieces for about 20-25 minutes, turning occasionally, until the internal temperature reaches 165°F (74°C) and the skin is charred and crispy.

5. Rest and Serve:

- Let the Jamaican Jerk Chicken rest for a few minutes before serving.

6. Enjoy:

- Serve the jerk chicken with traditional sides like rice and peas, coleslaw, or fried plantains. Enjoy the flavorful and spicy Jamaican Jerk Chicken!

This recipe captures the bold and spicy flavors of Jamaican jerk seasoning, creating a delicious and aromatic grilled chicken dish. Adjust the spice level according to your preference, and feel free to serve it with your favorite Caribbean-inspired sides.

Brazilian Churrasco Skewers

Ingredients:

For the Marinade:

- 2 pounds beef sirloin or flank steak, cut into 1-inch cubes
- 1/4 cup soy sauce
- 1/4 cup olive oil
- 4 cloves garlic, minced
- 2 tablespoons fresh parsley, chopped
- 1 tablespoon ground cumin
- 1 tablespoon paprika
- 1 teaspoon black pepper
- 1 teaspoon red pepper flakes (optional for heat)
- Juice of 1 lime

For the Skewers:

- Wooden or metal skewers (if using wooden skewers, soak them in water for 30 minutes before grilling)

Optional Toppings:

- Chimichurri sauce for serving
- Sliced limes for garnish

Instructions:

1. Prepare the Marinade:

- In a bowl, whisk together soy sauce, olive oil, minced garlic, chopped parsley, ground cumin, paprika, black pepper, red pepper flakes (if using), and lime juice.

2. Marinate the Meat:

- Place the beef cubes in a large, resealable plastic bag or a bowl.

- Pour the marinade over the meat, ensuring all pieces are well-coated. Seal the bag or cover the bowl and marinate in the refrigerator for at least 2 hours, preferably longer for more flavor.

3. Assemble the Skewers:

- Preheat your grill to medium-high heat.
- Thread the marinated beef cubes onto the skewers, leaving a little space between each piece.

4. Grill the Skewers:

- Grill the skewers for approximately 8-10 minutes, turning occasionally, until the meat is cooked to your desired level of doneness.

5. Rest and Serve:

- Let the Brazilian Churrasco Skewers rest for a few minutes before serving.

6. Optional: Chimichurri Sauce:

- Serve the skewers with chimichurri sauce on the side for an extra burst of flavor.

7. Garnish:

- Garnish with sliced limes for a fresh touch.

8. Enjoy:

- Serve these delicious Brazilian Churrasco Skewers as a main course with your favorite side dishes or as part of a barbecue feast!

These skewers are a wonderful representation of Brazilian barbecue culture, showcasing the bold and savory flavors of the marinade. They are perfect for grilling outdoors and bringing a taste of Brazil to your table.

Moroccan Spiced Lamb Kebabs

Ingredients:

For the Marinade:

- 1.5 pounds boneless lamb, cut into 1-inch cubes
- 3 tablespoons olive oil
- 3 cloves garlic, minced
- 1 teaspoon ground cumin
- 1 teaspoon ground coriander
- 1 teaspoon ground paprika
- 1 teaspoon ground cinnamon
- 1 teaspoon ground turmeric
- 1 teaspoon ground ginger
- 1 teaspoon ground cayenne pepper (adjust for heat preference)
- 1 teaspoon ground black pepper
- 1 teaspoon salt
- Juice of 1 lemon
- Zest of 1 lemon
- 2 tablespoons fresh cilantro, chopped

For the Kebabs:

- Wooden or metal skewers (if using wooden skewers, soak them in water for 30 minutes before grilling)
- Cherry tomatoes, red onion wedges, and bell peppers for skewering with the lamb

Instructions:

1. Prepare the Marinade:

- In a bowl, combine all the marinade ingredients: olive oil, minced garlic, ground cumin, ground coriander, ground paprika, ground cinnamon, ground turmeric, ground ginger, cayenne pepper, black pepper, salt, lemon juice, lemon zest, and chopped cilantro.

2. Marinate the Lamb:

- Place the lamb cubes in a large bowl or resealable plastic bag.
- Pour the marinade over the lamb, ensuring all pieces are well-coated. Seal the bag or cover the bowl and marinate in the refrigerator for at least 2 hours, or ideally overnight for maximum flavor.

3. Assemble the Kebabs:

- Preheat your grill to medium-high heat.
- Thread the marinated lamb cubes onto the skewers, alternating with cherry tomatoes, red onion wedges, and bell peppers.

4. Grill the Kebabs:

- Grill the kebabs for approximately 10-12 minutes, turning occasionally, until the lamb is cooked to your desired level of doneness and the vegetables are charred and tender.

5. Rest and Serve:

- Let the Moroccan Spiced Lamb Kebabs rest for a few minutes before serving.

6. Optional: Serve with Couscous:

- Serve the kebabs over a bed of couscous for a complete Moroccan-inspired meal.

7. Enjoy:

- Enjoy these flavorful and aromatic Moroccan Spiced Lamb Kebabs with your favorite sides and sauces!

This recipe brings the warm and exotic flavors of Moroccan spices to your grill, creating a delicious and satisfying dish. The combination of spices adds depth and richness to the succulent lamb, making it a perfect choice for a special meal or barbecue gathering.

Greek Souvlaki with Tzatziki

Ingredients:

- 1.5 pounds (about 700g) of your choice of meat (chicken, pork, or lamb), cut into bite-sized pieces
- 1/4 cup olive oil
- 3 cloves garlic, minced
- 1 teaspoon dried oregano
- 1 teaspoon dried thyme
- 1 teaspoon paprika
- Salt and pepper to taste
- Wooden skewers, soaked in water for at least 30 minutes

Instructions:

In a bowl, mix together the olive oil, minced garlic, oregano, thyme, paprika, salt, and pepper to create the marinade.
Add the bite-sized meat pieces to the marinade, ensuring they are well-coated. Cover the bowl and let it marinate in the refrigerator for at least 2 hours, or preferably overnight for more flavor.
Preheat your grill or grill pan to medium-high heat.
Thread the marinated meat onto the soaked wooden skewers.
Grill the skewers for about 10-15 minutes, turning occasionally, until the meat is cooked through and has a nice char.

Tzatziki Sauce:

Ingredients:

- 1 cup Greek yogurt
- 1 cucumber, grated and excess water squeezed out
- 2 cloves garlic, minced
- 1 tablespoon olive oil
- 1 tablespoon fresh dill, chopped
- 1 tablespoon fresh mint, chopped
- Salt and pepper to taste

Instructions:

In a bowl, combine the Greek yogurt, grated cucumber, minced garlic, olive oil, chopped dill, and mint. Mix well.

Season the Tzatziki with salt and pepper to taste. Refrigerate for at least 30 minutes before serving to allow the flavors to meld.

Serve the grilled Souvlaki skewers with a generous dollop of Tzatziki sauce on the side. You can also serve them in pita bread with sliced tomatoes, red onions, and lettuce for a complete and satisfying Greek meal. Enjoy!

Hawaiian Huli Huli Chicken

Ingredients:

- 4-6 bone-in, skin-on chicken thighs or other preferred chicken pieces

Marinade:

- 1/2 cup soy sauce
- 1/2 cup ketchup
- 1/3 cup brown sugar
- 1/4 cup chicken broth
- 1/4 cup pineapple juice
- 1/4 cup rice vinegar
- 2 tablespoons ginger, minced
- 2 tablespoons garlic, minced
- 1 tablespoon sesame oil
- 1 teaspoon Worcestershire sauce
- Pineapple slices (for garnish, optional)

Instructions:

In a bowl, whisk together all the marinade ingredients until the sugar is dissolved.

Place the chicken pieces in a large resealable plastic bag or a shallow dish. Pour about half of the marinade over the chicken, reserving the other half for basting and serving. Seal the bag or cover the dish and refrigerate for at least 2 hours, or preferably overnight, turning the chicken occasionally to ensure even marination.

Preheat your grill to medium-high heat.

Remove the chicken from the marinade and let any excess drip off. Discard the used marinade.

Grill the chicken for about 25-30 minutes, turning occasionally and basting with the reserved marinade during the last 10-15 minutes of cooking. Cook until the chicken reaches an internal temperature of 165°F (74°C) and has a nice caramelized glaze.

Optional: Grill pineapple slices for a few minutes on each side until they have grill marks.

Serve the Huli Huli Chicken hot, garnished with grilled pineapple slices if desired. You can also serve it with rice, coleslaw, or your favorite tropical sides.

Enjoy the tropical flavors of Hawaiian Huli Huli Chicken!

Mexican Carne Asada Tacos

Ingredients:

For the Carne Asada Marinade:

- 1.5 pounds (about 700g) flank or skirt steak
- Juice of 2 limes
- Juice of 1 orange
- 3 cloves garlic, minced
- 1/4 cup chopped fresh cilantro
- 1/4 cup olive oil
- 1 teaspoon ground cumin
- 1 teaspoon chili powder
- 1 teaspoon smoked paprika
- Salt and pepper to taste

For Serving:

- Small corn or flour tortillas
- Chopped onion and fresh cilantro (for garnish)
- Salsa or pico de gallo
- Lime wedges

Instructions:

In a bowl, whisk together the lime juice, orange juice, minced garlic, chopped cilantro, olive oil, cumin, chili powder, smoked paprika, salt, and pepper to create the marinade.

Place the steak in a shallow dish or a resealable plastic bag and pour the marinade over it. Make sure the steak is well-coated. Marinate in the refrigerator for at least 1-2 hours, or preferably overnight.

Preheat your grill to medium-high heat.

Remove the steak from the marinade and let any excess drip off. Season with additional salt and pepper if needed.

Grill the steak for about 4-6 minutes per side, depending on thickness, or until it reaches your desired level of doneness. Allow it to rest for a few minutes before slicing thinly against the grain.

While the steak is resting, warm the tortillas on the grill for about 30 seconds on each side.

Assemble your tacos by placing slices of carne asada on the warmed tortillas. Top with chopped onion, fresh cilantro, and your choice of salsa or pico de gallo. Serve the Carne Asada Tacos with lime wedges on the side.

Enjoy the delicious flavors of Mexican Carne Asada Tacos! Feel free to customize your tacos with additional toppings like guacamole, shredded cheese, or hot sauce.

Indian Tandoori Chicken

Ingredients:

For the Marinade:

- 1.5 pounds (about 700g) chicken pieces (drumsticks, thighs, or a combination)
- 1 cup plain yogurt
- 2 tablespoons ginger-garlic paste
- 1 tablespoon lemon juice
- 1 tablespoon ground cumin
- 1 tablespoon ground coriander
- 1 tablespoon paprika or Kashmiri red chili powder (for color)
- 1 teaspoon turmeric powder
- 1 teaspoon garam masala
- 1 teaspoon ground cinnamon
- 1 teaspoon ground cardamom
- Salt to taste
- 2 tablespoons vegetable oil

For Garnish:

- Fresh cilantro, chopped
- Lemon wedges

Instructions:

In a large bowl, mix together all the marinade ingredients until well combined. Make shallow cuts on the surface of the chicken pieces to allow the marinade to penetrate.
Coat the chicken pieces evenly with the marinade, making sure to get the mixture into the cuts. Cover the bowl and refrigerate for at least 4 hours, or overnight for best results.
Preheat your oven to the highest temperature setting (usually around 475°F/245°C). If you have a grill, you can also use it for an authentic smoky flavor.
If using an oven, place a wire rack on a baking sheet. Arrange the marinated chicken pieces on the rack, allowing any excess marinade to drip off.
Bake in the preheated oven for about 25-30 minutes or until the chicken is fully cooked, and the edges are charred. If grilling, cook over medium-high heat, turning occasionally until done.

Garnish the Tandoori Chicken with chopped cilantro and serve with lemon wedges on the side.

Enjoy the Tandoori Chicken on its own or with naan, rice, or a side of cooling raita.

Feel free to adjust the spice levels to suit your taste, and you can also add a few drops of red food coloring for that classic vibrant Tandoori color.

Turkish Adana Kebabs

Ingredients:

For the Kebab Mixture:

- 1.5 pounds (about 700g) ground lamb or a combination of lamb and beef
- 1 medium-sized onion, finely grated and excess liquid squeezed out
- 2 cloves garlic, minced
- 1 tablespoon tomato paste
- 1 tablespoon red pepper flakes (adjust to taste)
- 1 teaspoon ground cumin
- 1 teaspoon ground coriander
- 1 teaspoon sumac (optional)
- Salt and black pepper to taste

For Grilling:

- Skewers (metal or wooden, if using wooden skewers, soak them in water for at least 30 minutes)
- Olive oil (for brushing)

Instructions:

In a large bowl, combine the ground meat, grated onion, minced garlic, tomato paste, red pepper flakes, cumin, coriander, sumac (if using), salt, and black pepper. Mix the ingredients thoroughly until well combined.
Take a small portion of the meat mixture and shape it onto a skewer, pressing and molding it along the length of the skewer. Repeat until all the meat is used, and the skewers are formed.
Preheat your grill to medium-high heat.
Brush the kebabs with olive oil and place them on the preheated grill.
Grill the Adana Kebabs for about 12-15 minutes, turning occasionally, until they are cooked through and have a nice char on the outside.
Serve the kebabs with flatbread, rice, or a salad. You can also accompany them with yogurt sauce or tzatziki.
Garnish with chopped parsley and lemon wedges for extra flavor.

Enjoy the flavorful and spicy Turkish Adana Kebabs! Adjust the level of spiciness to suit your preference, and feel free to customize the sides according to your taste.

Thai Grilled Lemongrass Pork

Ingredients:

For the Marinade:

- 1.5 pounds (about 700g) pork shoulder or pork loin, thinly sliced

For the Marinade Paste:

- 3 stalks lemongrass, white part only, finely minced
- 4 cloves garlic, minced
- 1 shallot, minced
- 1 tablespoon ginger, minced
- 2 tablespoons fish sauce
- 2 tablespoons soy sauce
- 2 tablespoons oyster sauce
- 1 tablespoon honey or brown sugar
- 1 tablespoon sesame oil
- 1 teaspoon ground coriander
- 1 teaspoon ground cumin
- 1 teaspoon turmeric powder
- 1/2 teaspoon black pepper
- Lime wedges (for serving)

Instructions:

In a bowl, combine all the ingredients for the marinade paste - lemongrass, garlic, shallot, ginger, fish sauce, soy sauce, oyster sauce, honey or brown sugar, sesame oil, ground coriander, ground cumin, turmeric powder, and black pepper.
Place the thinly sliced pork in a large bowl and add the marinade paste. Mix well, ensuring that the pork is thoroughly coated. Cover the bowl and let it marinate in the refrigerator for at least 2 hours, or preferably overnight.
Preheat your grill to medium-high heat.
Thread the marinated pork slices onto skewers, allowing excess marinade to drip off.
Grill the lemongrass pork skewers for about 8-10 minutes, turning occasionally, until the pork is cooked through and has a nice char on the outside.
Serve the grilled lemongrass pork skewers with lime wedges on the side for squeezing over the meat.

Enjoy the Thai Grilled Lemongrass Pork on its own, with rice, or in lettuce wraps for a lighter option.

This dish combines the unique flavors of lemongrass with other savory and aromatic ingredients, resulting in a deliciously grilled Thai-inspired pork dish.

Peruvian Anticuchos (Grilled Beef Heart)

Ingredients:

For the Marinade:

- 1.5 pounds (about 700g) beef heart, cleaned and cut into bite-sized cubes
- 1/4 cup aji panca paste (Peruvian red pepper paste), or substitute with aji amarillo paste
- 3 cloves garlic, minced
- 1 teaspoon ground cumin
- 1 teaspoon dried oregano
- 1/2 cup red wine vinegar
- 1/4 cup vegetable oil
- Salt and pepper to taste

For Skewering:

- Wooden skewers, soaked in water for at least 30 minutes

For Serving:

- Huancaina sauce (optional, for dipping)
- Boiled potatoes (optional)

Instructions:

In a bowl, combine the aji panca paste, minced garlic, ground cumin, dried oregano, red wine vinegar, vegetable oil, salt, and pepper to create the marinade. Add the beef heart cubes to the marinade, ensuring they are well-coated. Cover the bowl and let it marinate in the refrigerator for at least 4 hours, or preferably overnight for richer flavor.
Preheat your grill to medium-high heat.
Thread the marinated beef heart cubes onto the soaked wooden skewers.
Grill the anticuchos for about 8-10 minutes, turning occasionally, until the meat is cooked through and has a nice char on the outside.
Serve the Peruvian Anticuchos with huancaina sauce for dipping and boiled potatoes if desired.
Enjoy the unique and flavorful taste of Peruvian Anticuchos!

Note: If beef heart is not readily available or you prefer a milder flavor, you can also use beef sirloin or another cut of beef for this recipe. The marinade will still impart delicious Peruvian flavors to the meat.

Italian Grilled Bruschetta Chicken

Ingredients:

For the Grilled Chicken:

- 4 boneless, skinless chicken breasts
- 2 tablespoons olive oil
- 2 cloves garlic, minced
- 1 teaspoon dried oregano
- 1 teaspoon dried basil
- Salt and black pepper to taste

For the Bruschetta Topping:

- 4 medium-sized tomatoes, diced
- 3 tablespoons fresh basil, chopped
- 2 cloves garlic, minced
- 2 tablespoons balsamic vinegar
- 2 tablespoons extra-virgin olive oil
- Salt and black pepper to taste

For Serving:

- Freshly grated Parmesan cheese
- Balsamic glaze (optional)
- Fresh basil leaves for garnish

Instructions:

Preheat your grill to medium-high heat.
In a bowl, mix together the olive oil, minced garlic, dried oregano, dried basil, salt, and black pepper to create the marinade for the chicken.
Coat the chicken breasts with the marinade, making sure they are well covered. Let them marinate for at least 15-20 minutes.
Grill the chicken breasts for about 6-8 minutes per side or until fully cooked. Cooking times may vary depending on the thickness of the chicken. Ensure the internal temperature reaches 165°F (74°C).
While the chicken is grilling, prepare the bruschetta topping. In a bowl, combine diced tomatoes, chopped fresh basil, minced garlic, balsamic vinegar, extra-virgin olive oil, salt, and black pepper. Mix well.

Once the chicken is done, remove it from the grill and let it rest for a few minutes.
Top each grilled chicken breast with a generous spoonful of the bruschetta mixture.
Sprinkle freshly grated Parmesan cheese over the bruschetta topping.
Optionally, drizzle balsamic glaze over the chicken for extra flavor.
Garnish with fresh basil leaves and serve immediately.

Enjoy this Italian Grilled Bruschetta Chicken with a side of your favorite vegetables, pasta, or a simple green salad. It's a light and flavorful dish that's perfect for a summer meal.

South African Boerewors Sausage

Ingredients:

- 2 pounds (about 900g) beef, pork, or a combination, finely ground
- 1 large onion, finely chopped
- 2 cloves garlic, minced
- 2 teaspoons salt
- 1 teaspoon black pepper
- 1 teaspoon ground coriander
- 1 teaspoon ground allspice
- 1 teaspoon ground nutmeg
- 1 teaspoon ground cloves
- 1 teaspoon dried thyme
- 1 tablespoon Worcestershire sauce
- 1 tablespoon vinegar (malt or wine vinegar)
- Sausage casings

Instructions:

Soak the sausage casings in warm water according to the package instructions.

In a large mixing bowl, combine the ground meat, chopped onion, minced garlic, salt, black pepper, coriander, allspice, nutmeg, cloves, thyme, Worcestershire sauce, and vinegar. Mix the ingredients thoroughly.

Attach a sausage stuffing nozzle to a sausage stuffer or a meat grinder.

Thread the soaked casings onto the sausage stuffer nozzle, leaving a bit of an overhang.

Stuff the sausage casings with the meat mixture, making sure not to overfill and allowing some space for twisting into individual sausages.

Twist the sausages into 6-8 inch links, depending on your preference.

Refrigerate the sausages for at least a few hours or overnight to allow the flavors to meld.

Before cooking, let the sausages come to room temperature for about 30 minutes.

Grill the Boerewors sausages over medium-high heat for approximately 15-20 minutes, turning occasionally, until cooked through and nicely browned.

Serve the Boerewors sausages hot with your favorite side dishes or as part of a traditional South African "braai" (barbecue).

Boerewors sausages are often enjoyed with sides like chakalaka, pap (a type of maize porridge), or potato salad. They are a delicious representation of South African cuisine and are perfect for a barbecue or any festive gathering.

Spanish Grilled Seafood Paella

Ingredients:

For the Marinade:

- 1 pound (about 450g) large shrimp, peeled and deveined
- 1 pound (about 450g) mussels, cleaned and debearded
- 1 pound (about 450g) squid, cleaned and sliced into rings
- 1/4 cup olive oil
- 3 cloves garlic, minced
- 1 teaspoon smoked paprika
- 1 teaspoon sweet paprika
- 1 teaspoon dried oregano
- Salt and black pepper to taste
- Juice of 1 lemon

For the Paella:

- 2 cups bomba or short-grain rice
- 4 cups chicken or seafood broth (or a combination)
- 1 large onion, finely chopped
- 1 red bell pepper, diced
- 4 tomatoes, grated
- 1/2 teaspoon saffron threads, soaked in 2 tablespoons warm water
- 1 teaspoon smoked paprika
- Salt and black pepper to taste
- 1/4 cup olive oil
- Lemon wedges for serving

Instructions:

In a bowl, combine the shrimp, mussels, and squid with olive oil, minced garlic, smoked paprika, sweet paprika, dried oregano, salt, pepper, and lemon juice. Allow the seafood to marinate for at least 30 minutes.

Preheat your grill to medium-high heat.

In a large paella pan or a wide, shallow pan suitable for the grill, heat olive oil. Add chopped onion and diced red bell pepper. Sauté until the vegetables are softened.

Add grated tomatoes to the pan and cook until the mixture becomes a thick sauce.

Stir in the rice, saffron with its soaking water, smoked paprika, salt, and black pepper. Mix well to coat the rice with the flavorful ingredients.

Pour in the chicken or seafood broth, spreading it evenly over the rice. Allow the mixture to come to a boil.

Arrange the marinated seafood over the rice, distributing it evenly.

Place the paella pan on the preheated grill and close the lid. Grill for about 20-25 minutes or until the rice is cooked, and the seafood is cooked through.

Check for a golden crust, known as "socarrat," at the bottom of the paella. If necessary, increase the heat for the last few minutes to achieve this.

Remove the paella from the grill and let it rest for a few minutes before serving.

Serve the Grilled Seafood Paella hot, garnished with lemon wedges.

Enjoy this Spanish Grilled Seafood Paella as a delightful and communal dish perfect for sharing with friends and family. It captures the essence of Spanish cuisine with its rich flavors and textures.

Filipino Inihaw na Baboy (Grilled Pork Belly)

Ingredients:

- 1.5 pounds (about 700g) pork belly, thinly sliced
- 1/2 cup soy sauce
- 1/4 cup ketchup
- 1/4 cup calamansi juice or lemon juice
- 1/4 cup brown sugar
- 1 tablespoon garlic, minced
- 1 teaspoon black pepper
- 1 teaspoon salt
- Bamboo skewers, soaked in water for at least 30 minutes

Instructions:

In a bowl, combine soy sauce, ketchup, calamansi juice (or lemon juice), brown sugar, minced garlic, black pepper, and salt. Mix well to create the marinade.

Place the thinly sliced pork belly in a large resealable plastic bag or a shallow dish.

Pour the marinade over the pork, making sure each slice is well-coated. Seal the bag or cover the dish and let it marinate in the refrigerator for at least 2 hours, or preferably overnight.

Preheat your grill to medium-high heat.

Thread the marinated pork slices onto the soaked bamboo skewers.

Grill the pork belly skewers for about 5-7 minutes per side or until fully cooked and has a nice char.

While grilling, baste the pork belly with the remaining marinade to enhance the flavor and keep the meat moist.

Once cooked, transfer the Inihaw na Baboy to a serving platter.

Serve hot with steamed rice and your favorite dipping sauce, like a mixture of soy sauce and calamansi juice.

Enjoy the smoky and savory goodness of Inihaw na Baboy, a beloved Filipino grilled pork dish that's perfect for gatherings and celebrations.

Lebanese Grilled Kafta Kebabs

Ingredients:

For the Kafta Mixture:

- 1 pound (about 450g) ground lamb or a lamb/beef mix
- 1 medium onion, finely grated and excess liquid squeezed out
- 2 tablespoons fresh parsley, finely chopped
- 2 tablespoons fresh mint, finely chopped
- 2 cloves garlic, minced
- 1 teaspoon ground cumin
- 1 teaspoon ground coriander
- 1/2 teaspoon ground allspice
- 1/2 teaspoon cayenne pepper (optional, for heat)
- Salt and black pepper to taste

For Grilling:

- Skewers (metal or wooden, if using wooden skewers, soak them in water for at least 30 minutes)
- Olive oil (for brushing)
- Lemon wedges (for serving)

Instructions:

In a large mixing bowl, combine ground lamb (or lamb/beef mix), grated onion, chopped parsley, chopped mint, minced garlic, ground cumin, ground coriander, ground allspice, cayenne pepper (if using), salt, and black pepper. Mix well until all ingredients are evenly distributed.
Preheat your grill to medium-high heat.
Divide the kafta mixture into portions and shape them onto skewers, molding the meat around the skewer to form elongated kebabs.
Brush the kafta kebabs with olive oil.
Grill the kebabs for about 10-15 minutes, turning occasionally, until they are fully cooked and have a nice char on the outside.
Serve the Lebanese Grilled Kafta Kebabs hot with lemon wedges on the side.

These delicious kebabs can be served with flatbread, rice, or a simple salad. You can also pair them with a traditional garlic sauce or tzatziki for added flavor. Enjoy the authentic taste of Lebanese cuisine with these flavorful grilled kafta kebabs.

Chinese Char Siu Pork

Ingredients:

For the Marinade:

- 1.5 pounds (about 700g) pork shoulder or pork loin, thinly sliced or cut into strips

For the Marinade:

- 3 tablespoons hoisin sauce
- 3 tablespoons soy sauce
- 2 tablespoons honey
- 1 tablespoon oyster sauce
- 1 tablespoon Chinese rice wine or dry sherry
- 1 tablespoon brown sugar
- 1 teaspoon five-spice powder
- 1 teaspoon sesame oil
- 2 cloves garlic, minced
- 1 tablespoon grated ginger
- Red food coloring (optional, for the traditional red color)

Instructions:

In a bowl, combine all the marinade ingredients - hoisin sauce, soy sauce, honey, oyster sauce, Chinese rice wine, brown sugar, five-spice powder, sesame oil, minced garlic, grated ginger, and red food coloring if using.
Place the thinly sliced or cut pork in a large resealable plastic bag or a shallow dish.
Pour the marinade over the pork, making sure each piece is well-coated. Seal the bag or cover the dish and let it marinate in the refrigerator for at least 4 hours, or preferably overnight.
Preheat your oven to 375°F (190°C).
Thread the marinated pork onto skewers or place them on a wire rack set over a baking sheet to allow air circulation.
Bake the Char Siu in the preheated oven for about 25-30 minutes, turning occasionally and basting with the marinade, until the pork is cooked through and has a nice caramelized glaze.
Optional: Broil for an additional 2-3 minutes to get a slightly charred appearance.
Slice the Char Siu into thin pieces and serve hot.

Enjoy the Chinese Char Siu Pork as a main dish with rice, noodles, or in sandwiches. The sweet and savory flavor with a hint of spice from the five-spice powder makes it a flavorful and satisfying dish.

Australian Grilled Kangaroo

Ingredients:

- 1 pound (about 450g) kangaroo steaks or fillets
- Olive oil
- Salt and pepper to taste
- Optional marinade: garlic, herbs, soy sauce, or balsamic vinegar

Instructions:

Prepare the Kangaroo Steaks:
- If using a marinade, combine your choice of ingredients (garlic, herbs, soy sauce, balsamic vinegar) in a bowl.
- Place the kangaroo steaks in a shallow dish and pour the marinade over them. Cover and let them marinate for at least 30 minutes, or overnight in the refrigerator if time allows.

Preheat the Grill:
- Preheat your grill to medium-high heat. Ensure the grill grates are clean and lightly oiled to prevent sticking.

Season the Kangaroo:
- Remove the kangaroo steaks from the marinade and let any excess drip off. Pat them dry with paper towels.
- Drizzle olive oil over the steaks and season with salt and pepper.

Grill the Kangaroo:
- Place the kangaroo steaks on the preheated grill. Grill for approximately 2-3 minutes per side for medium-rare, or longer if you prefer your meat more well-done. Kangaroo meat cooks quickly, so keep a close eye on it to avoid overcooking.

Rest the Meat:
- Once cooked to your liking, remove the kangaroo steaks from the grill and let them rest for a few minutes. This helps retain their juices.

Slice and Serve:
- Slice the kangaroo steaks against the grain into thin strips.
- Serve the grilled kangaroo steaks with your choice of side dishes, such as roasted vegetables, salad, or couscous.

Note: Kangaroo meat is very lean, so be cautious not to overcook it, as it can become tough.

Aim for medium-rare to medium doneness for the best texture and flavor.

Grilled kangaroo is a unique and flavorful dish, and it's essential to treat it with care during cooking to appreciate its natural taste and tenderness.

Vietnamese Grilled Lemongrass Beef

Ingredients:

For the Marinade:

- 1.5 pounds (about 700g) beef sirloin or flank steak, thinly sliced
- 3 stalks lemongrass, white part only, finely minced
- 3 cloves garlic, minced
- 2 shallots, minced
- 3 tablespoons fish sauce
- 2 tablespoons soy sauce
- 2 tablespoons oyster sauce
- 2 tablespoons sugar
- 1 tablespoon honey or molasses
- 1 tablespoon sesame oil
- 1 teaspoon ground black pepper

For Grilling:

- Skewers (metal or wooden, if using wooden skewers, soak them in water for at least 30 minutes)
- Vegetable oil (for brushing)

Instructions:

Prepare the Marinade:
- In a bowl, combine minced lemongrass, minced garlic, minced shallots, fish sauce, soy sauce, oyster sauce, sugar, honey or molasses, sesame oil, and ground black pepper. Mix well to create the marinade.

Marinate the Beef:
- Add the thinly sliced beef to the marinade, ensuring each piece is well-coated. Cover and refrigerate for at least 2 hours, or overnight for optimal flavor.

Thread the Skewers:
- Preheat your grill to medium-high heat.
- Thread the marinated beef slices onto the skewers, shaking off excess marinade.

Grill the Lemongrass Beef:
- Brush the grill grates with vegetable oil to prevent sticking.

- Grill the skewers for about 2-3 minutes per side, or until the beef is cooked to your desired doneness and has a nice char.

Serve Hot:
- Remove the skewers from the grill and let them rest for a couple of minutes.
- Serve the grilled lemongrass beef skewers hot, either on their own or with rice vermicelli, rice, or as part of a Vietnamese-inspired noodle bowl.

Garnish (Optional):
- Garnish with chopped fresh cilantro, mint, or basil.
- Serve with dipping sauce, such as nuoc cham (Vietnamese dipping sauce).

Enjoy the Vietnamese Grilled Lemongrass Beef as a tasty and aromatic dish that captures the essence of Vietnamese cuisine. The lemongrass imparts a refreshing and citrusy flavor to the beef, making it a delightful choice for grilling.

Russian Shashlik (Marinated Grilled Skewers)

Ingredients:

For the Marinade:

- 2 pounds (about 900g) pork or lamb, cut into cubes
- 1 large onion, finely chopped
- 2 cloves garlic, minced
- 1/4 cup vegetable oil
- 1/4 cup white wine vinegar
- 2 tablespoons soy sauce
- 1 tablespoon Dijon mustard
- 1 teaspoon paprika
- 1 teaspoon ground cumin
- 1 teaspoon dried thyme
- Salt and black pepper to taste

For Grilling:

- Skewers (metal or wooden, if using wooden skewers, soak them in water for at least 30 minutes)
- Vegetable oil (for brushing)
- Optional: Sliced vegetables (bell peppers, onions, mushrooms) for skewering with the meat

Instructions:

Prepare the Marinade:
- In a bowl, mix together the chopped onion, minced garlic, vegetable oil, white wine vinegar, soy sauce, Dijon mustard, paprika, ground cumin, dried thyme, salt, and black pepper.

Marinate the Meat:
- Place the cubed meat in a large resealable plastic bag or a shallow dish.
- Pour the marinade over the meat, ensuring that all pieces are well-coated. Seal the bag or cover the dish and refrigerate for at least 4 hours, or overnight for better flavor.

Skewering:
- Preheat your grill to medium-high heat.

- Thread the marinated meat onto skewers, alternating with optional sliced vegetables if desired.

Grill the Shashlik:
- Brush the grill grates with vegetable oil to prevent sticking.
- Grill the skewers for about 15-20 minutes, turning occasionally, or until the meat is cooked through and has a nice char on the outside.

Serve Hot:
- Remove the skewers from the grill and let them rest for a couple of minutes.
- Serve the Russian Shashlik hot with your favorite side dishes, such as rice, flatbread, or a simple salad.

Enjoy the flavorful and tender Russian Shashlik as a delicious grilled dish that's perfect for outdoor gatherings or any occasion. The marinated meat imparts a rich and savory taste that is sure to be a hit.

Jamaican Escovitch Fish

Ingredients:

For the Fried Fish:

- 2 pounds (about 900g) whole snapper, grunt, or any firm white fish, cleaned and scaled
- Salt and black pepper to taste
- 1 cup all-purpose flour, for coating
- Vegetable oil, for frying

For the Escovitch Sauce:

- 1 cup thinly sliced carrots
- 1 cup thinly sliced onions
- 1 cup thinly sliced bell peppers (assorted colors)
- 2 Scotch bonnet peppers, thinly sliced (seeds removed for less heat if desired)
- 1 cup white vinegar
- 1/2 cup water
- 2 teaspoons sugar
- 1 teaspoon salt
- 1 teaspoon whole allspice
- 4 sprigs thyme

Instructions:

Prepare and Fry the Fish:
- Clean and scale the fish, then cut slits on both sides. Pat the fish dry with paper towels.
- Season the fish with salt and black pepper, ensuring the seasoning gets into the slits.
- Dredge the fish in flour, shaking off excess.
- Heat vegetable oil in a large frying pan over medium-high heat.
- Fry the fish for about 5-7 minutes per side or until golden brown and cooked through. Drain on paper towels.

Prepare the Escovitch Sauce:
- In a separate pan, combine the sliced carrots, onions, bell peppers, Scotch bonnet peppers, white vinegar, water, sugar, salt, and whole allspice.

- Bring the mixture to a boil and simmer for 5-7 minutes or until the vegetables are slightly softened but still vibrant.
- Add thyme sprigs and stir.

Assemble:
- Arrange the fried fish on a serving platter.
- Pour the hot escovitch sauce over the fried fish, ensuring the vegetables are evenly distributed.

Serve:
- Serve the Jamaican Escovitch Fish hot, garnished with additional fresh thyme if desired.
- It pairs well with traditional Jamaican side dishes like fried plantains, rice and peas, or bammy.

Enjoy the bold and spicy flavors of Jamaican Escovitch Fish, a dish that reflects the vibrant and diverse culinary heritage of Jamaica.

Argentine Provoleta (Grilled Cheese)

Ingredients:

- 1 round of Provolone cheese (about 8-10 ounces)
- 1 tablespoon olive oil
- 2 teaspoons dried oregano
- 1 teaspoon crushed red pepper flakes (optional)
- 1 teaspoon dried thyme
- 1 teaspoon dried rosemary
- 2 cloves garlic, minced
- Sliced baguette or crackers, for serving

Instructions:

Prepare the Grill:
- Preheat your grill to medium-high heat.

Prepare the Provolleta:
- Place the round of Provolone cheese on a cast-iron skillet or a heatproof dish suitable for the grill.

Season the Cheese:
- Drizzle the top of the Provolone with olive oil.
- Sprinkle minced garlic, dried oregano, crushed red pepper flakes (if using), dried thyme, and dried rosemary evenly over the cheese.

Grill the Provoleta:
- Place the skillet or dish on the preheated grill.
- Close the grill lid and cook for about 8-10 minutes or until the Provolone is melted and bubbly, with a golden crust on top.

Serve:
- Carefully remove the hot skillet or dish from the grill.
- Serve the Argentine Provoleta immediately with sliced baguette or crackers for dipping.

Enjoy:
- Invite your guests to scoop out the gooey, flavorful cheese with bread or crackers.

Argentine Provoleta is often enjoyed as a shared appetizer or during social gatherings. It's a simple yet satisfying dish that showcases the rich and savory flavors of melted Provolone cheese with aromatic herbs and spices.

Mexican Street Corn (Elote)

Ingredients:

- 4 ears of corn, husked
- 1/4 cup mayonnaise
- 1/4 cup sour cream
- 1/2 cup crumbled cotija cheese (or feta cheese as a substitute)
- 1 teaspoon chili powder (adjust to taste)
- 1/4 cup finely chopped fresh cilantro
- Lime wedges for serving

Instructions:

Grill the Corn:
- Preheat your grill to medium-high heat.
- Grill the husked corn for about 10-15 minutes, turning occasionally, until it has a nice char and is cooked through.

Prepare the Elote Sauce:
- In a bowl, mix together mayonnaise, sour cream, crumbled cotija cheese, chili powder, and chopped cilantro. Adjust the chili powder to your desired level of spiciness.

Coat the Corn:
- Once the corn is grilled, use a brush or a spoon to coat each ear of corn generously with the elote sauce.

Serve:
- Sprinkle additional crumbled cotija cheese and chili powder on top for garnish.
- Serve the Mexican Street Corn hot with lime wedges on the side.

Enjoy:
- Squeeze fresh lime juice over the corn before taking a bite.

Mexican Street Corn is a flavorful and satisfying treat that perfectly balances the sweetness of the corn with the creamy, tangy, and spicy elote sauce. It's a fantastic dish to enjoy during barbecues, picnics, or as a side dish for Mexican-themed meals.

Greek Grilled Halloumi Cheese

Ingredients:

- 1 block of halloumi cheese (about 8-10 ounces)
- 2 tablespoons olive oil
- 1 tablespoon fresh lemon juice
- 1 teaspoon dried oregano
- Black pepper, to taste
- Optional: Fresh herbs (such as mint or basil) for garnish

Instructions:

Preheat the Grill:
- Preheat your grill to medium-high heat.

Prepare the Halloumi:
- Cut the halloumi cheese into thick slices, about 1/2 inch to 3/4 inch in thickness.

Marinate the Halloumi:
- In a small bowl, whisk together olive oil, fresh lemon juice, dried oregano, and black pepper.
- Brush both sides of the halloumi slices with the marinade.

Grill the Halloumi:
- Place the halloumi slices directly on the preheated grill grates.
- Grill for about 2-3 minutes per side, or until grill marks appear, and the cheese is warmed through.

Serve:
- Remove the grilled halloumi from the grill and transfer it to a serving plate.

Garnish (Optional):
- Garnish the grilled halloumi with fresh herbs, such as mint or basil.

Enjoy:
- Serve the Greek Grilled Halloumi Cheese warm as an appetizer or part of a mezze platter.

Grilled halloumi is often enjoyed on its own, but you can also serve it with a side of fresh tomatoes, olives, and crusty bread. The salty and firm texture of halloumi makes it a delightful addition to summer grilling sessions or as a light and flavorful snack.

Brazilian Picanha Steak

Ingredients:

- 2-3 pounds (about 1-1.5 kg) Picanha (top sirloin cap), fat cap intact
- Coarse salt (rock salt or sea salt)
- Optional: Garlic powder or minced garlic
- Optional: Black pepper

Instructions:

Prepare the Picanha:
- If the Picanha comes with a thick layer of fat, score the fat in a diamond pattern. Make shallow cuts to allow the fat to render and crisp during grilling.
- Optionally, rub the meat with garlic powder or minced garlic and black pepper for added flavor.

Season with Salt:
- Generously season the Picanha with coarse salt. Brazilian Picanha is traditionally seasoned only with salt to enhance its natural beef flavor.

Prepare the Grill:
- Preheat your grill to medium-high heat. For an authentic Brazilian experience, you can use a charcoal grill.

Skewering the Picanha:
- Cut the Picanha into thick strips, about 2 inches wide.
- Skewer the Picanha strips onto metal skewers, making sure to thread them through the fat layer.

Grill the Picanha:
- Place the skewers on the preheated grill, fat side down.
- Grill for about 10-15 minutes, turning occasionally, or until the fat is rendered, and the meat is cooked to your desired doneness. Picanha is often enjoyed medium-rare to medium.

Rest and Slice:
- Allow the grilled Picanha to rest for a few minutes to let the juices redistribute.
- Slice the Picanha against the grain into thin strips.

Serve:
- Serve the Brazilian Picanha Steak hot, traditionally with sides like farofa (toasted cassava flour), rice, black beans, and Brazilian salsa (vinaigrette).

Brazilian Picanha is a favorite at churrascarias (Brazilian steakhouses), and this simple recipe allows you to enjoy the authentic flavors of this popular cut at home. The crispy fat cap and seasoned meat make it a delicious and memorable dish.

Thai Grilled Coconut Milk Marinated Chicken

Ingredients:

For the Marinade:

1.5 pounds (about 700g) boneless, skinless chicken thighs or chicken breasts

1 cup coconut milk

3 tablespoons soy sauce

2 tablespoons fish sauce

2 tablespoons brown sugar

2 tablespoons minced lemongrass

2 tablespoons minced garlic

2 tablespoons minced shallots

1 tablespoon grated ginger

1 tablespoon lime zest

1 teaspoon ground coriander

1 teaspoon ground cumin

1 teaspoon turmeric powder

1 teaspoon chili flakes (adjust to taste)

Fresh cilantro for garnish

Instructions:

Prepare the Marinade:

In a bowl, whisk together coconut milk, soy sauce, fish sauce, brown sugar, minced lemongrass, minced garlic, minced shallots, grated ginger, lime zest, ground coriander, ground cumin, turmeric powder, and chili flakes.

Marinate the Chicken:

Place the chicken thighs or breasts in a shallow dish or a resealable plastic bag.

Pour the marinade over the chicken, ensuring each piece is well-coated.

Cover the dish or seal the bag and refrigerate for at least 4 hours, or preferably overnight, to allow the flavors to meld.

Preheat the Grill:

Preheat your grill to medium-high heat.

Grill the Chicken:

Remove the chicken from the marinade, letting excess marinade drip off.

Grill the chicken for about 5-7 minutes per side or until fully cooked and has a nice char on the outside.

Garnish and Serve:

Garnish the grilled chicken with fresh cilantro.

Serve the Thai Grilled Coconut Milk Marinated Chicken hot with rice, noodles, or your favorite side dishes.

Enjoy this Thai-inspired dish that brings together the creaminess of coconut milk and the aromatic blend of Thai spices. It's perfect for a barbecue or a flavorful weeknight meal.

Turkish Grilled Eggplant Kebabs

Ingredients:

- 2 large eggplants
- 2 bell peppers (red, green, or a combination), cut into chunks
- 1 large red onion, cut into chunks
- Cherry tomatoes (optional)
- Olive oil for brushing

For the Marinade:

- 1/4 cup olive oil
- 2 tablespoons tomato paste
- 2 cloves garlic, minced
- 1 teaspoon ground cumin
- 1 teaspoon paprika
- 1 teaspoon dried oregano
- Salt and black pepper to taste
- Juice of 1 lemon

Instructions:

Prepare the Marinade:
- In a bowl, whisk together olive oil, tomato paste, minced garlic, ground cumin, paprika, dried oregano, salt, black pepper, and lemon juice. This will be the marinade for your kebabs.

Prepare the Vegetables:
- Cut the eggplants into thick rounds or chunks.
- Place the eggplant chunks, bell pepper chunks, red onion chunks, and cherry tomatoes (if using) in a large bowl.

Marinate the Vegetables:
- Pour the marinade over the vegetables, making sure they are well-coated. Allow them to marinate for at least 30 minutes, allowing the flavors to meld.

Assemble the Kebabs:
- Thread the marinated vegetables onto skewers, alternating between eggplant, bell pepper, and onion. You can add cherry tomatoes between the chunks.

Preheat the Grill:

- Preheat your grill to medium-high heat.

Grill the Kebabs:
- Brush the vegetable kebabs with olive oil.
- Grill the kebabs for about 10-15 minutes, turning occasionally, or until the vegetables are tender and have a nice char.

Serve:
- Remove the kebabs from the grill and place them on a serving platter.

Enjoy:
- Serve the Turkish Grilled Eggplant Kebabs hot, either on their own or with flatbread and a side of yogurt or a flavorful sauce.

These Turkish Grilled Eggplant Kebabs are a delicious and healthy option that highlights the natural flavors of the vegetables. They are perfect for a barbecue or as a side dish for a Mediterranean-inspired meal.

Korean Grilled Miso-Glazed Salmon

Ingredients:

For the Miso Glaze:

- 1/4 cup white miso paste
- 2 tablespoons soy sauce
- 2 tablespoons mirin (Japanese sweet rice wine)
- 1 tablespoon honey
- 1 tablespoon rice vinegar
- 1 teaspoon grated fresh ginger
- 2 cloves garlic, minced
- 1 tablespoon sesame oil
- 4 salmon fillets

Optional Garnish:

- Sesame seeds
- Sliced green onions
- Thinly sliced red chili (for a spicy kick)

Instructions:

Prepare the Miso Glaze:
- In a bowl, whisk together white miso paste, soy sauce, mirin, honey, rice vinegar, grated ginger, minced garlic, and sesame oil until well combined.

Marinate the Salmon:
- Place the salmon fillets in a shallow dish or a resealable plastic bag.
- Pour the miso glaze over the salmon, ensuring each fillet is well-coated.
- Marinate the salmon in the refrigerator for at least 30 minutes, allowing the flavors to infuse.

Preheat the Grill:
- Preheat your grill to medium-high heat.

Grill the Salmon:
- Remove the salmon from the marinade and shake off excess.
- Place the salmon fillets on the preheated grill, skin side down.
- Grill for about 4-5 minutes per side, or until the salmon is cooked through and has a nice char on the outside.

Optional: Baste with Glaze:

- Optionally, you can baste the salmon with additional miso glaze during the grilling process for extra flavor.

Garnish and Serve:
- Transfer the grilled miso-glazed salmon to a serving platter.
- Garnish with sesame seeds, sliced green onions, and thinly sliced red chili if desired.

Enjoy:
- Serve the Korean Grilled Miso-Glazed Salmon hot, paired with steamed rice or your favorite side dishes.

This Korean-inspired grilled salmon offers a perfect balance of sweet, savory, and umami flavors, making it a delightful and sophisticated dish for any occasion.

Indian Grilled Paneer Tikka

Ingredients:

For the Marinade:

- 250g paneer, cut into cubes
- 1 cup thick yogurt
- 1 tablespoon ginger-garlic paste
- 1 tablespoon gram flour (besan)
- 1 tablespoon lemon juice
- 1 teaspoon red chili powder
- 1 teaspoon turmeric powder
- 1 teaspoon garam masala
- 1 teaspoon cumin powder
- 1 teaspoon coriander powder
- Salt to taste
- 1 tablespoon vegetable oil

For the Vegetables (Optional):

- Bell peppers, onions, and cherry tomatoes, cut into chunks

For Grilling:

- Skewers (metal or wooden, if using wooden skewers, soak them in water for at least 30 minutes)
- Vegetable oil for brushing

Instructions:

Prepare the Marinade:
- In a bowl, combine thick yogurt, ginger-garlic paste, gram flour, lemon juice, red chili powder, turmeric powder, garam masala, cumin powder, coriander powder, salt, and vegetable oil. Mix well to form a smooth marinade.

Marinate the Paneer:
- Add the paneer cubes to the marinade, ensuring each piece is well-coated.
- Cover and refrigerate for at least 1-2 hours, or preferably overnight, to let the flavors meld.

Assemble the Skewers:
- If using vegetables, thread marinated paneer cubes alternately with bell peppers, onions, and cherry tomatoes onto skewers.

Preheat the Grill:
- Preheat your grill to medium-high heat.

Grill the Paneer Tikka:
- Brush the grill grates with vegetable oil to prevent sticking.
- Place the skewers on the preheated grill and cook for about 8-10 minutes, turning occasionally, or until the paneer is golden brown and has a nice char.

Serve Hot:
- Remove the paneer tikka skewers from the grill and transfer them to a serving platter.

Garnish (Optional):
- Garnish with freshly chopped coriander and lemon wedges.

Enjoy:
- Serve the Indian Grilled Paneer Tikka hot with mint chutney or your favorite dipping sauce.

Grilled Paneer Tikka is a flavorful and appetizing dish that can be enjoyed as a starter, snack, or even as part of a larger meal. The smoky flavor from the grill and the aromatic spices make it a popular choice in Indian cuisine.

Peruvian Grilled Chicken with Aji Verde

Ingredients:

For the Grilled Chicken:

- 4 boneless, skinless chicken breasts or thighs
- 3 cloves garlic, minced
- 1 teaspoon ground cumin
- 1 teaspoon paprika
- 1 teaspoon dried oregano
- 1 teaspoon ground black pepper
- 1 teaspoon salt
- 2 tablespoons vegetable oil
- Juice of 2 limes

For the Aji Verde Sauce:

- 1 cup fresh cilantro leaves, packed
- 1/2 cup fresh parsley leaves, packed
- 1 jalapeño pepper, seeds removed (adjust for spice level)
- 2 cloves garlic
- 2 tablespoons chopped green onions
- 2 tablespoons mayonnaise
- 1 tablespoon Dijon mustard
- 1 tablespoon white wine vinegar
- Salt and pepper to taste

Instructions:

Marinate the Chicken:
- In a bowl, combine minced garlic, ground cumin, paprika, dried oregano, black pepper, salt, vegetable oil, and lime juice.
- Coat the chicken breasts or thighs with the marinade, ensuring each piece is well-coated.
- Cover and refrigerate for at least 30 minutes, or longer for better flavor.

Prepare the Aji Verde Sauce:
- In a blender or food processor, combine cilantro, parsley, jalapeño, garlic, green onions, mayonnaise, Dijon mustard, white wine vinegar, salt, and pepper.

- Blend until you achieve a smooth and creamy consistency. Adjust salt and pepper to taste.

Preheat the Grill:
- Preheat your grill to medium-high heat.

Grill the Chicken:
- Remove the chicken from the marinade and shake off excess.
- Grill the chicken for about 6-8 minutes per side, or until fully cooked and has a nice char.

Serve:
- Transfer the grilled chicken to a serving platter.
- Drizzle the Aji Verde sauce over the chicken or serve it on the side.

Garnish (Optional):
- Garnish with additional chopped cilantro or green onions.

Enjoy:
- Serve the Peruvian Grilled Chicken with Aji Verde hot, accompanied by rice, quinoa, or your favorite side dishes.

This dish captures the bold and flavorful taste of Peruvian cuisine, with the grilled chicken and zesty Aji Verde sauce providing a delicious combination of heat and freshness.

Moroccan Grilled Vegetable Platter

Ingredients:

For the Marinade:

- 1/4 cup olive oil
- 2 tablespoons lemon juice
- 2 teaspoons ground cumin
- 2 teaspoons ground coriander
- 1 teaspoon smoked paprika
- 1 teaspoon ground turmeric
- 1 teaspoon ground cinnamon
- 1 teaspoon ground ginger
- Salt and black pepper to taste

For the Grilled Vegetables:

- Zucchini, sliced lengthwise
- Eggplant, sliced into rounds
- Bell peppers, sliced into strips
- Cherry tomatoes, on the vine
- Red onions, sliced into rounds
- Mushrooms, cleaned and halved
- Any other preferred vegetables

For Garnish:

- Fresh cilantro, chopped
- Fresh mint, chopped
- Lemon wedges

Instructions:

Prepare the Marinade:
- In a bowl, whisk together olive oil, lemon juice, ground cumin, ground coriander, smoked paprika, ground turmeric, ground cinnamon, ground ginger, salt, and black pepper.

Marinate the Vegetables:
- Place the sliced vegetables in a large bowl.

- Pour the marinade over the vegetables, tossing to ensure they are evenly coated.
- Let the vegetables marinate for at least 30 minutes, allowing the flavors to meld.

Preheat the Grill:
- Preheat your grill to medium-high heat.

Grill the Vegetables:
- Arrange the marinated vegetables on the preheated grill grates.
- Grill the vegetables for 5-7 minutes per side or until they are tender and have beautiful grill marks.

Assemble the Platter:
- Arrange the grilled vegetables on a large serving platter.

Garnish:
- Sprinkle chopped fresh cilantro and mint over the grilled vegetables.
- Place lemon wedges on the platter for a fresh citrusy touch.

Serve:
- Serve the Moroccan Grilled Vegetable Platter as a side dish or a vegetarian main course.
- Optionally, you can serve it with couscous or quinoa for a complete meal.

This Moroccan Grilled Vegetable Platter is not only visually appealing but also bursting with the bold flavors of North African spices. It makes for a perfect dish for gatherings, barbecues, or as a colorful addition to your dinner table.

Italian Grilled Octopus

Ingredients:

- 2 pounds of octopus, cleaned and tentacles separated
- 1/4 cup extra-virgin olive oil
- 4 cloves garlic, minced
- 1 teaspoon dried oregano
- 1 teaspoon crushed red pepper flakes (adjust to taste)
- Salt and black pepper to taste
- Juice of 1 lemon
- Fresh parsley, chopped, for garnish

Instructions:

Preparation of Octopus:
- If you haven't already, clean the octopus by removing the beak and internal organs.
- Rinse the octopus under cold water.
- Tenderize the octopus by either boiling it for about 20-30 minutes or by using a meat mallet to pound it gently.

Marination:
- In a bowl, mix together olive oil, minced garlic, oregano, crushed red pepper flakes, salt, and black pepper.
- Place the octopus in a shallow dish and coat it evenly with the marinade.
- Cover the dish and let the octopus marinate in the refrigerator for at least 30 minutes or up to a few hours for more flavor.

Grilling:
- Preheat your grill to medium-high heat.
- Remove the octopus from the refrigerator and let it come to room temperature.
- Grill the octopus for about 4-5 minutes per side, or until it develops a nice char and is cooked through. Be careful not to overcook, as it can become tough.

Finishing Touch:
- Transfer the grilled octopus to a serving platter.
- Squeeze fresh lemon juice over the grilled octopus for a burst of citrus flavor.

- Garnish with chopped fresh parsley.

Serving:
- Serve the Italian grilled octopus as a appetizer or main dish.
- You can also drizzle a bit more olive oil over the top before serving for added richness.

Enjoy your delicious Italian grilled octopus!

South African Braai Broodjie (Grilled Cheese Sandwich)

Ingredients:

8 slices of fresh white bread
Butter, softened
1 large tomato, thinly sliced
1 large onion, thinly sliced into rings
2 cups grated cheddar cheese
Salt and pepper to taste
Apricot or peach chutney (optional)

Instructions:

Preheat the Braai (Barbecue):
- Heat your braai or barbecue to medium-high heat.

Butter the Bread:
- Spread a thin layer of softened butter on one side of each slice of bread.

Assemble the Sandwiches:
- On the non-buttered side of four slices of bread, place a layer of sliced tomatoes and onions.
- Sprinkle a generous amount of grated cheddar cheese over the tomatoes and onions.
- Season with salt and pepper to taste.
- Optionally, add a dollop of apricot or peach chutney for extra flavor.

Create Sandwiches:
- Place the remaining four slices of bread on top, buttered side facing out, to form sandwiches.

Grill the Braai Broodjies:
- Place the assembled sandwiches on the preheated braai or barbecue grill.
- Grill for about 3-5 minutes per side or until the bread is golden brown, and the cheese is melted and gooey.

Serve:
- Once the Braai Broodjies are grilled to perfection, remove them from the braai.
- Allow them to cool for a minute before slicing them into halves or quarters.

- Serve the grilled cheese sandwiches as a delightful side dish at your South African braai.

Braai Broodjies are a delicious and easy addition to any barbecue or outdoor gathering, and they showcase the flavors of South African cuisine. Enjoy!

Spanish Grilled Piquillo Peppers

Ingredients:

1 jar of Piquillo peppers, drained
Extra-virgin olive oil
Salt, to taste
Optional: Garlic cloves, minced, for added flavor
Optional: Fresh parsley, chopped, for garnish

Instructions:

Preheat the Grill:
- Preheat your grill to medium-high heat.

Prepare Piquillo Peppers:
- Drain the Piquillo peppers from the jar and pat them dry with a paper towel.

Grilling:
- Lightly brush each pepper with extra-virgin olive oil to prevent sticking and enhance flavor.
- Place the peppers on the preheated grill, turning them occasionally, until they are heated through and have grill marks (usually about 3-5 minutes).

Optional Garlic Infusion:
- If you want to add a garlic flavor, you can mince garlic and mix it with some olive oil. Brush this garlic-infused oil over the peppers before grilling.

Seasoning:
- Sprinkle the grilled Piquillo peppers with a pinch of salt to enhance the flavors.

Garnish:
- Optional: Garnish the grilled peppers with freshly chopped parsley for added freshness and color.

Serve:
- Arrange the grilled Piquillo peppers on a serving platter.

These grilled Piquillo peppers can be served warm or at room temperature. They make a wonderful tapas dish or a flavorful side to accompany a variety of Spanish meals. Enjoy the smoky, charred goodness of these delicious grilled peppers!

Filipino Bangus (Grilled Milkfish)

Grilled Bangus, or milkfish, is a popular and delicious dish in Filipino cuisine. Here's a simple recipe to prepare Grilled Bangus:

Ingredients:

2 whole Bangus (milkfish), scaled, cleaned, and butterflied
1 cup soy sauce
1/2 cup calamansi juice (or lemon juice as a substitute)
3 cloves garlic, minced
1 teaspoon ground black pepper
2 tablespoons brown sugar
Salt, to taste
Banana leaves for wrapping (optional)
Cooking oil for brushing

Instructions:

Prepare the Marinade:
- In a bowl, combine soy sauce, calamansi juice (or lemon juice), minced garlic, ground black pepper, brown sugar, and salt. Mix well to dissolve the sugar and salt.

Marinate the Bangus:
- Place the cleaned and butterflied Bangus in a large, shallow dish or a resealable plastic bag.
- Pour the marinade over the Bangus, making sure it's well-coated. Marinate for at least 30 minutes to allow the flavors to penetrate the fish.

Preheat the Grill:
- Preheat your grill to medium-high heat.

Prepare Banana Leaves (Optional):
- If using banana leaves, lightly brush them with oil and quickly pass them over an open flame to make them pliable.

Wrap and Grill:
- Lay the marinated Bangus on the banana leaves if using, or directly on the grill grates.

- Grill the Bangus for about 15-20 minutes per side or until the fish is cooked through and has a nice char. Baste with the marinade during grilling.

Serve:
- Once the Bangus is fully grilled, transfer it to a serving platter.
- Serve the Grilled Bangus with steamed rice and your favorite dipping sauce (such as soy sauce with calamansi or vinegar with garlic and soy sauce).

Grilled Bangus is a flavorful and satisfying dish that captures the essence of Filipino cuisine. Enjoy the smoky aroma and delicious taste of this grilled milkfish!

Lebanese Grilled Garlic Shrimp

Ingredients:

- 1 pound large shrimp, peeled and deveined
- 4 cloves garlic, minced
- 1/4 cup fresh lemon juice
- 1/4 cup extra-virgin olive oil
- 1 teaspoon ground cumin
- 1 teaspoon paprika
- 1/2 teaspoon cayenne pepper (adjust to taste)
- Salt and black pepper, to taste
- Fresh parsley, chopped, for garnish
- Lemon wedges, for serving

Instructions:

Marinate the Shrimp:
- In a bowl, combine minced garlic, fresh lemon juice, extra-virgin olive oil, ground cumin, paprika, cayenne pepper, salt, and black pepper.
- Add the peeled and deveined shrimp to the marinade, ensuring they are well-coated. Allow the shrimp to marinate for at least 30 minutes in the refrigerator.

Preheat the Grill:
- Preheat your grill to medium-high heat.

Skewer the Shrimp:
- Thread the marinated shrimp onto skewers, leaving some space between each shrimp.

Grilling:
- Place the shrimp skewers on the preheated grill and cook for about 2-3 minutes per side or until the shrimp are opaque and have grill marks.

Garnish and Serve:
- Remove the shrimp skewers from the grill and place them on a serving platter.
- Sprinkle chopped fresh parsley over the grilled shrimp for a burst of color and freshness.
- Serve the Lebanese Grilled Garlic Shrimp with lemon wedges on the side.

Optional: Serve with a Side:

- You can serve the grilled shrimp over a bed of couscous or with a side of a refreshing salad.

This Lebanese Grilled Garlic Shrimp is not only flavorful but also quick and easy to prepare. Enjoy the delicious taste of the Mediterranean with this simple and tasty recipe!

Chinese Grilled Eggplant with Garlic Sauce

Ingredients:

For the Grilled Eggplant:

- 2 medium-sized Chinese or Japanese eggplants
- 2 tablespoons soy sauce
- 1 tablespoon sesame oil
- 2 tablespoons vegetable oil
- Salt and black pepper, to taste

For the Garlic Sauce:

- 4 cloves garlic, minced
- 2 tablespoons soy sauce
- 1 tablespoon rice vinegar
- 1 tablespoon sugar
- 1 teaspoon sesame oil
- Red pepper flakes (optional, for heat)
- Green onions, chopped, for garnish

Instructions:

Prepare the Eggplant:
- Wash the eggplants and cut off the ends. Slice them in half lengthwise.

Preheat the Grill:
- Preheat your grill to medium-high heat.

Brush with Oil:
- In a small bowl, mix together soy sauce, sesame oil, and vegetable oil.
- Brush the eggplant halves with the oil mixture on both sides. Season with salt and black pepper.

Grilling the Eggplant:
- Place the eggplant halves on the preheated grill, cut side down.
- Grill for about 5-7 minutes until the eggplant is tender and has grill marks.
- Flip the eggplant and grill for an additional 5-7 minutes until fully cooked.

Prepare the Garlic Sauce:
- While the eggplant is grilling, prepare the garlic sauce. In a small bowl, combine minced garlic, soy sauce, rice vinegar, sugar, sesame oil, and red pepper flakes (if using). Mix well.

Assemble:

- Once the eggplant is done, transfer it to a serving plate.
- Drizzle the garlic sauce over the grilled eggplant.

Garnish and Serve:
- Garnish with chopped green onions for freshness and color.
- Serve the Chinese Grilled Eggplant with Garlic Sauce as a delicious side dish.

This dish pairs well with steamed rice or as part of a larger Chinese-inspired meal. The combination of smoky grilled eggplant and savory garlic sauce creates a delightful and satisfying flavor profile. Enjoy!

Australian Grilled Barramundi

Ingredients:

- 4 Barramundi fillets (about 6-8 ounces each)
- 2 tablespoons olive oil
- 2 tablespoons lemon juice
- 2 cloves garlic, minced
- 1 teaspoon dried oregano
- 1 teaspoon paprika
- Salt and black pepper, to taste
- Lemon wedges, for serving
- Fresh herbs (such as parsley or dill) for garnish

Instructions:

Preheat the Grill:
- Preheat your grill to medium-high heat.

Prepare the Marinade:
- In a small bowl, whisk together olive oil, lemon juice, minced garlic, dried oregano, paprika, salt, and black pepper.

Marinate the Barramundi:
- Place the Barramundi fillets in a shallow dish or a resealable plastic bag.
- Pour the marinade over the fillets, ensuring they are well-coated. Let them marinate for about 15-30 minutes to absorb the flavors.

Grilling:
- Remove the Barramundi fillets from the marinade and shake off any excess.
- Place the fillets on the preheated grill, skin side down, if they have skin.
- Grill for approximately 4-6 minutes per side, depending on the thickness of the fillets, or until the fish is opaque and easily flakes with a fork.

Garnish and Serve:
- Transfer the grilled Barramundi to a serving platter.
- Garnish with fresh herbs and serve with lemon wedges on the side.

Optional: Grilled Vegetables or Salad:
- Serve the Grilled Barramundi over a bed of grilled vegetables or with a side of fresh salad for a complete meal.

This Australian Grilled Barramundi is a simple yet flavorful dish that lets the natural taste of the fish shine through. Enjoy the light and flaky texture of Barramundi with the added smokiness from the grill!

Vietnamese Grilled Pork Banh Mi

Ingredients:

For the Grilled Pork:

- 1 pound pork shoulder or pork tenderloin, thinly sliced
- 3 cloves garlic, minced
- 2 tablespoons soy sauce
- 1 tablespoon fish sauce
- 1 tablespoon honey or sugar
- 1 tablespoon vegetable oil
- 1 teaspoon lemongrass, minced (optional)
- Black pepper, to taste

For the Banh Mi:

- Baguettes or French rolls
- Mayonnaise
- Maggi seasoning sauce or soy sauce
- Pickled daikon and carrot (do chua)
- Fresh cilantro sprigs
- Sliced cucumber
- Sliced jalapeños
- Optional: Sriracha or chili sauce for added heat

Instructions:

Grilled Pork:

Marinate the Pork:
- In a bowl, combine minced garlic, soy sauce, fish sauce, honey (or sugar), vegetable oil, lemongrass (if using), and black pepper.
- Add the thinly sliced pork to the marinade, ensuring each piece is well-coated. Marinate for at least 30 minutes, or preferably longer for more flavor.

Grilling:
- Preheat your grill or grill pan to medium-high heat.
- Thread the marinated pork slices onto skewers or grill them directly.
- Grill the pork for 2-3 minutes per side or until fully cooked and slightly charred.

Banh Mi Assembly:

Prepare the Baguette:
- Cut the baguettes or French rolls in half, lengthwise.

Spread Condiments:
- Spread mayonnaise on one side of the bread and drizzle Maggi seasoning sauce or soy sauce on the other side.

Add Grilled Pork:
- Place a generous amount of grilled pork on the bottom half of the bread.

Layer Vegetables:
- Top the pork with pickled daikon and carrot, fresh cilantro sprigs, sliced cucumber, and jalapeños.

Optional: Add Heat:
- If you like it spicy, add a drizzle of Sriracha or your favorite chili sauce.

Assemble and Serve:
- Place the top half of the baguette on the assembled ingredients, pressing down gently.
- Cut the Banh Mi into smaller portions if desired.

Enjoy your homemade Vietnamese Grilled Pork Banh Mi, a perfect blend of savory, sweet, and spicy flavors!

Russian Grilled Potatoes with Dill

Ingredients:

- 4 large potatoes, washed and scrubbed
- 3 tablespoons olive oil
- 2 tablespoons fresh dill, chopped
- 2 cloves garlic, minced
- Salt and black pepper, to taste
- Sour cream, for serving (optional)

Instructions:

Preheat the Grill:
- Preheat your grill to medium-high heat.

Prepare the Potatoes:
- Slice the potatoes into rounds, about 1/4 to 1/2 inch thick. Parboil the potato slices in salted water for about 5 minutes or until they are slightly tender but not fully cooked.

Create the Marinade:
- In a bowl, combine olive oil, chopped dill, minced garlic, salt, and black pepper. Mix well to create the marinade.

Marinate the Potatoes:
- Toss the parboiled potato slices in the marinade, ensuring they are well-coated.

Grilling:
- Place the marinated potato slices directly on the preheated grill grates.
- Grill for about 5-7 minutes per side, or until the potatoes are golden brown and cooked through. Be sure to check for grill marks.

Garnish:
- Once the potatoes are done, transfer them to a serving platter.
- Sprinkle extra chopped dill on top as a garnish.

Serve:
- Serve the grilled potatoes with a dollop of sour cream on the side, if desired.

This Russian Grilled Potatoes with Dill recipe is a delightful way to enjoy the smoky flavor from the grill combined with the freshness of dill. It makes for a tasty and comforting side dish that complements a variety of main courses. Enjoy!

Jamaican Grilled Jerk Portobello Mushrooms

Ingredients:

For the Jerk Marinade:

- 3-4 large portobello mushrooms, stems removed
- 2 tablespoons soy sauce
- 2 tablespoons olive oil
- 2 tablespoons dark brown sugar
- 1 tablespoon thyme leaves, chopped
- 2 teaspoons ground allspice
- 1-2 teaspoons Scotch bonnet pepper, minced (adjust to taste)
- 1 teaspoon ground cinnamon
- 1 teaspoon ground nutmeg
- 4 green onions, chopped
- 4 cloves garlic, minced
- 1 tablespoon fresh ginger, grated
- Juice of 1 lime
- Salt and black pepper, to taste

For Grilling:

- Cooking spray or additional oil for the grill grates

Instructions:

Prepare the Jerk Marinade:
- In a bowl, combine all the ingredients for the jerk marinade - soy sauce, olive oil, dark brown sugar, thyme, allspice, Scotch bonnet pepper, cinnamon, nutmeg, green onions, garlic, ginger, lime juice, salt, and black pepper. Mix well to form a paste.

Marinate the Portobello Mushrooms:
- Clean the portobello mushrooms and remove the stems.
- Generously coat each mushroom with the jerk marinade, ensuring they are well-covered. Allow them to marinate for at least 30 minutes, or longer for more flavor.

Preheat the Grill:
- Preheat your grill to medium-high heat.

Prepare the Grill Grates:

- Brush the grill grates with cooking spray or oil to prevent sticking.

Grilling:
- Place the marinated portobello mushrooms on the preheated grill.
- Grill for about 5-7 minutes per side or until the mushrooms are tender and have grill marks.

Serve:
- Transfer the grilled jerk portobello mushrooms to a serving plate.
- Optionally, garnish with additional chopped green onions or fresh thyme.

Optional: Serve with Sides:
- Serve the Jamaican Grilled Jerk Portobello Mushrooms with your favorite sides, such as rice, salad, or grilled vegetables.

Enjoy these flavorful and spicy Jamaican Grilled Jerk Portobello Mushrooms as a delicious vegetarian dish with a Caribbean twist!

Argentine Grilled Sausage with Chimichurri

Ingredients:

For the Grilled Sausage:

- 1 pound Argentine-style sausages (such as chorizo or morcilla)
- Olive oil for brushing

For the Chimichurri Sauce:

- 1 cup fresh parsley, finely chopped
- 4 cloves garlic, minced
- 1/2 cup extra-virgin olive oil
- 2 tablespoons red wine vinegar
- 1 tablespoon dried oregano
- 1 teaspoon red pepper flakes (adjust to taste)
- Salt and black pepper, to taste

Instructions:

Grilled Sausage:

   Preheat the Grill:
   - Preheat your grill to medium-high heat.

   Grilling Sausage:
   - Place the Argentine-style sausages on the preheated grill.
   - Grill the sausages for about 15-20 minutes, turning occasionally, until they are cooked through and have a nice char on the outside.

   Brush with Olive Oil:
   - During the last few minutes of grilling, brush the sausages with olive oil to enhance flavor and prevent drying.

   Chimichurri Sauce:
   - While the sausages are grilling, prepare the chimichurri sauce.
   - In a bowl, combine finely chopped parsley, minced garlic, extra-virgin olive oil, red wine vinegar, dried oregano, red pepper flakes, salt, and black pepper. Mix well.

   Serve:
   - Once the sausages are cooked, transfer them to a serving platter.
   - Serve the grilled sausages with a generous drizzle of chimichurri sauce.

   Optional: Side Accompaniments:
   - Serve the Argentine Grilled Sausage with Chimichurri alongside crusty bread, grilled vegetables, or a simple salad.

This dish captures the essence of Argentine barbecue traditions, with the rich, smoky flavor of the grilled sausages complemented by the zesty and herby chimichurri sauce. Enjoy the bold and delicious flavors of Argentine cuisine!

Greek Grilled Feta with Honey

Ingredients:

- 1 block of feta cheese (about 8 ounces)
- 1 tablespoon extra-virgin olive oil
- 1 tablespoon honey
- Freshly ground black pepper, to taste
- Optional: Fresh herbs (such as oregano or thyme) for garnish
- Optional: Sliced baguette or pita for serving

Instructions:

Preheat the Grill:
- Preheat your grill to medium-high heat.

Prepare the Feta:
- Cut the block of feta into a thick slice or keep it whole, depending on your preference.

Grilling:
- Brush the feta slice with extra-virgin olive oil on both sides to prevent sticking.
- Place the feta on the preheated grill and cook for about 2-3 minutes per side, or until it develops grill marks and becomes slightly soft.

Transfer to Serving Plate:
- Carefully remove the grilled feta from the grill and transfer it to a serving plate.

Drizzle with Honey:
- Drizzle honey over the top of the grilled feta. You can adjust the amount of honey based on your sweetness preference.

Season with Black Pepper:
- Sprinkle freshly ground black pepper over the feta for an extra kick.

Garnish:
- Optionally, garnish the grilled feta with fresh herbs like oregano or thyme for added flavor and visual appeal.

Serve:
- Serve the Greek Grilled Feta with Honey immediately while it's warm. You can enjoy it as is or spread it onto sliced baguette or pita.

This dish is a delightful combination of textures and flavors, and it makes for a fantastic appetizer for a Greek-inspired meal or as part of a mezze platter. Enjoy the creamy goodness of grilled feta paired with the sweet touch of honey!

Turkish Grilled Quail

Ingredients:

For the Marinade:

- 8 quails, cleaned and spatchcocked
- 1/4 cup olive oil
- 3 cloves garlic, minced
- 1 lemon, juiced
- 2 teaspoons ground cumin
- 2 teaspoons paprika
- 1 teaspoon ground coriander
- 1 teaspoon ground cinnamon
- Salt and black pepper, to taste

For Serving:

- Fresh lemon wedges
- Chopped fresh parsley

Instructions:

Prepare the Quail:
- Clean the quails thoroughly and pat them dry with paper towels.
- Using kitchen shears, spatchcock the quails by cutting along one side of the backbone and then the other. Flatten the quails to ensure even cooking.

Prepare the Marinade:
- In a bowl, whisk together olive oil, minced garlic, lemon juice, ground cumin, paprika, ground coriander, ground cinnamon, salt, and black pepper to create the marinade.

Marinate the Quail:
- Place the spatchcocked quails in a shallow dish and brush them generously with the marinade. Ensure each quail is well-coated.
- Cover the dish and let the quails marinate in the refrigerator for at least 2 hours, or preferably overnight for more flavor.

Preheat the Grill:
- Preheat your grill to medium-high heat.

Grilling:
- Remove the quails from the marinade and let any excess drip off.

- Grill the quails for about 5-7 minutes per side, or until they are cooked through and have a nice char on the outside.

Serve:
- Transfer the grilled quails to a serving platter.
- Garnish with fresh lemon wedges and chopped parsley.

Optional: Accompaniments:
- Serve the Turkish Grilled Quail with your favorite side dishes, such as rice, grilled vegetables, or a simple salad.

This Turkish Grilled Quail recipe showcases the rich and aromatic flavors of the marinade, creating a delicious and tender dish. Enjoy this Turkish delicacy with family and friends!

Korean Grilled Gochujang Ribs

Ingredients:

For the Marinade:

- 2 racks of baby back ribs
- 1/2 cup gochujang (Korean red chili paste)
- 1/4 cup soy sauce
- 3 tablespoons honey
- 3 tablespoons mirin (rice wine)
- 3 cloves garlic, minced
- 1 tablespoon grated ginger
- 1 tablespoon sesame oil
- 1 tablespoon rice vinegar
- 1 teaspoon black pepper

For Garnish:

- Sesame seeds
- Sliced green onions

Instructions:

Prepare the Ribs:
- Trim excess fat from the ribs and remove the membrane from the back of the racks for better flavor absorption.

Make the Marinade:
- In a bowl, combine gochujang, soy sauce, honey, mirin, minced garlic, grated ginger, sesame oil, rice vinegar, and black pepper. Whisk the ingredients together until well combined.

Marinate the Ribs:
- Place the racks of ribs in a large dish or a resealable plastic bag. Pour the marinade over the ribs, ensuring they are well coated. Marinate in the refrigerator for at least 4 hours, preferably overnight for maximum flavor.

Grill the Ribs:

- Preheat your grill to medium-high heat. Remove the ribs from the marinade and let them come to room temperature for about 30 minutes.
- Grill the ribs over indirect heat for approximately 30-40 minutes, turning occasionally, until the meat is cooked through and has a nice char.

Baste with Marinade:
- During the last 15 minutes of grilling, baste the ribs with some of the remaining marinade, using a brush. Make sure to reserve some marinade for serving.

Garnish and Serve:
- Once the ribs are cooked through and have a beautiful caramelized crust, remove them from the grill. Sprinkle sesame seeds and sliced green onions on top. Serve with the reserved marinade on the side for dipping.

Enjoy your delicious Korean Grilled Gochujang Ribs! They pair well with steamed rice, kimchi, and other Korean side dishes for a complete and satisfying meal.

Italian Grilled Swordfish with Lemon

Ingredients:

- 4 swordfish steaks (about 6-8 ounces each)
- 1/4 cup extra-virgin olive oil
- 3 tablespoons fresh lemon juice
- Zest of one lemon
- 2 cloves garlic, minced
- 1 teaspoon dried oregano
- 1 teaspoon dried thyme
- Salt and black pepper to taste
- Lemon wedges for serving
- Chopped fresh parsley for garnish (optional)

Instructions:

Prepare the Marinade:
- In a bowl, whisk together the extra-virgin olive oil, fresh lemon juice, lemon zest, minced garlic, dried oregano, dried thyme, salt, and black pepper.

Marinate the Swordfish:
- Place the swordfish steaks in a shallow dish or a resealable plastic bag. Pour the marinade over the steaks, ensuring they are well coated. Allow the fish to marinate in the refrigerator for at least 30 minutes. If possible, marinate for up to 2 hours for better flavor absorption.

Preheat the Grill:
- Preheat your grill to medium-high heat. Make sure the grates are clean and lightly oiled to prevent sticking.

Grill the Swordfish:
- Remove the swordfish steaks from the marinade and let any excess drip off. Place the steaks on the preheated grill and cook for about 4-5 minutes per side, or until the fish is opaque and flakes easily with a fork.

Baste with Marinade:
- While grilling, baste the swordfish with the remaining marinade using a brush. This adds extra flavor and helps keep the fish moist.

Serve:
- Once the swordfish is cooked through, transfer it to a serving platter. Garnish with chopped fresh parsley if desired. Serve hot with lemon wedges on the side.

This Italian Grilled Swordfish with Lemon pairs well with a simple salad, grilled vegetables, or a side of pasta. It's a light and refreshing dish that is perfect for a summertime meal. Enjoy!

Brazilian Grilled Pineapple with Cinnamon

Ingredients:

- 1 whole pineapple, peeled, cored, and sliced into rings
- 1/4 cup brown sugar
- 1 teaspoon ground cinnamon
- Cooking spray or oil for grilling

Instructions:

Prepare the Pineapple:
- Peel the pineapple and remove the core. Slice the pineapple into rings, each about 1/2 to 1 inch thick.

Prepare the Cinnamon Sugar Mixture:
- In a small bowl, mix together the brown sugar and ground cinnamon to create a cinnamon sugar mixture.

Preheat the Grill:
- Preheat your grill to medium-high heat. Make sure the grates are clean and lightly oiled to prevent sticking.

Coat the Pineapple:
- Lightly spray or brush both sides of each pineapple ring with cooking spray or oil. This helps prevent sticking and promotes a nice caramelization on the grill.

Grill the Pineapple:
- Place the pineapple rings directly on the preheated grill. Grill for about 2-3 minutes per side, or until you see grill marks and the pineapple begins to caramelize.

Cinnamon Sugar Coating:
- During the last minute of grilling, sprinkle the cinnamon sugar mixture over each side of the pineapple rings. Allow the sugar to melt and create a sweet, slightly crispy coating.

Serve:
- Remove the grilled pineapple from the grill and arrange the slices on a serving platter. Optionally, you can sprinkle additional cinnamon sugar on top for extra sweetness. Serve the grilled pineapple warm.

This Brazilian Grilled Pineapple with Cinnamon is a delightful combination of smoky, grilled flavor and sweet, spiced goodness. It can be enjoyed on its own or served with a scoop of vanilla ice cream for an extra indulgence. Enjoy!

Indian Grilled Tandoori Naan

Ingredients:

- 2 cups all-purpose flour
- 1 teaspoon active dry yeast
- 1 teaspoon sugar
- 1/2 teaspoon salt
- 1/4 teaspoon baking powder
- 2 tablespoons plain yogurt
- 1 tablespoon vegetable oil
- 2/3 cup warm water (approximately)

For Tandoori Marinade:

- 2 tablespoons plain yogurt
- 1 tablespoon melted ghee or butter
- 1 teaspoon garlic paste
- 1 teaspoon ginger paste
- 1 teaspoon ground cumin
- 1 teaspoon ground coriander
- 1/2 teaspoon turmeric
- 1/2 teaspoon smoked paprika (for color)
- Salt to taste
- Chopped fresh cilantro for garnish (optional)

Instructions:

Prepare the Dough:

In a small bowl, combine warm water, sugar, and yeast. Let it sit for about 5-10 minutes until frothy.
In a large mixing bowl, combine flour, salt, and baking powder. Make a well in the center.
Pour the activated yeast mixture into the well. Add yogurt and vegetable oil.
Gradually incorporate the dry ingredients into the wet ingredients, mixing well.
Add more water as needed to form a soft, elastic dough.

Knead the dough on a floured surface for about 5-7 minutes until smooth. Place the dough in a lightly oiled bowl, cover it with a damp cloth, and let it rest in a warm place for 1-2 hours or until it doubles in size.

Prepare the Tandoori Marinade:

In a bowl, mix together yogurt, melted ghee or butter, garlic paste, ginger paste, cumin, coriander, turmeric, smoked paprika, and salt. This is your tandoori marinade.

Grilling the Naan:

Preheat your grill to medium-high heat.
Punch down the risen dough and divide it into golf ball-sized portions.
Roll each portion into a thin, oval or round shape, about 1/4 inch thick.
Brush one side of each naan with the tandoori marinade.
Place the naan, marinade side down, directly on the grill grates. Cook for 2-3 minutes until bubbles form and the bottom is golden brown.
Brush the top side with the tandoori marinade, then flip the naan. Cook for an additional 2-3 minutes until the other side is golden brown.
Remove from the grill, sprinkle with chopped cilantro if desired, and serve warm.

Grilled Tandoori Naan is a wonderful accompaniment to various Indian dishes or can be enjoyed on its own with some yogurt or chutney. It's a versatile and flavorful bread that adds a special touch to your grilled meals.

Thai Grilled Green Curry Chicken Skewers

Ingredients:

For the Green Curry Marinade:

- 1 cup coconut milk
- 2 tablespoons green curry paste
- 2 tablespoons soy sauce
- 1 tablespoon fish sauce
- 1 tablespoon brown sugar
- 1 tablespoon lime juice
- 2 cloves garlic, minced
- 1 tablespoon fresh cilantro, chopped
- 1 tablespoon lemongrass, finely chopped (optional)
- 1 teaspoon grated ginger
- Salt and pepper to taste

For the Chicken Skewers:

- 1.5 lbs boneless, skinless chicken thighs, cut into bite-sized pieces
- Bamboo skewers, soaked in water for at least 30 minutes

For Serving (Optional):

- Thai sweet chili sauce
- Chopped fresh cilantro
- Lime wedges

Instructions:

Prepare the Marinade:
- In a bowl, whisk together coconut milk, green curry paste, soy sauce, fish sauce, brown sugar, lime juice, minced garlic, chopped cilantro, lemongrass (if using), grated ginger, salt, and pepper. This is your green curry marinade.

Marinate the Chicken:
- Place the chicken pieces in a resealable plastic bag or a shallow dish. Pour the green curry marinade over the chicken, ensuring it is well-coated.

- Marinate in the refrigerator for at least 1-2 hours, or overnight for maximum flavor.

Preheat the Grill:
- Preheat your grill to medium-high heat.

Skewer the Chicken:
- Thread the marinated chicken pieces onto the soaked bamboo skewers.

Grill the Chicken Skewers:
- Grill the chicken skewers for about 5-7 minutes per side, or until the chicken is fully cooked and has a nice char from the grill. Baste the chicken with any leftover marinade during grilling for extra flavor.

Serve:
- Remove the chicken skewers from the grill and arrange them on a serving platter. Optionally, drizzle with additional lime juice and garnish with chopped cilantro. Serve with Thai sweet chili sauce on the side and lime wedges.

These Thai Grilled Green Curry Chicken Skewers are perfect as an appetizer, main course, or part of a barbecue spread. The combination of the aromatic green curry marinade and the smoky grilled flavor creates a mouthwatering dish that's sure to be a hit. Enjoy!

www.ingramcontent.com/pod-product-compliance
Lightning Source LLC
LaVergne TN
LVHW081607060526
838201LV00054B/2127